THE
NIGHT BEFORE CHRISTMAS
IN
NEWFOUNDLAND

*Have a
Merry Christmas
Dec 25/99.

Proper ting!

Sincerely,
Uncle Al*

DEDICATION

Dedicated to my family
and to the good people of
Newfoundland who enjoy their
own special and unique brand
of humour, in other words
– Newfoundlanders.

ISBN 0-9690904-4-7

First Published 1984
Second Edition 1985
Third Edition 1986
Fourth Edition 1987
Fifth Edition 1988
Sixth Edition 1995

Al Clouston
P.O. Box 5922
St. John's, Nfld. A1C 5X4

Printed in Canada by Webcom Limited

Twas d'night afore Christmas
Down 'ere in Newfoundland
An' dere was h'ice an' big snowdrifts
A plenty on 'and.

Wit' d'kids
All a sleepin'
H'up stairs
In d'loft
An' Mudder in d'kitchen — Cookin' h'up
a big scoff.

Den I was cuttin' some
Splits fer d'stove
An' Mudder was bakin' some bread—
Jus' four loaves
Wit' peas puddin' an' cabbage
Some spuds an' carn beef
Jus' tinkin' about it
Sure t'will be a fine feast.

Den down be d'warf
Dere arose some
     big clatter,
I t'ought dat
Garge Murphy
fell h'off
d'flake ladder.

I runs to d'door
Like d'clap of a bell
Caught me toe
in the rug …

An' be jumpins
I fell.

H'as I gawked in d'garden
And h'out on d'bay
B'y d'cat got me tongue
I 'ad nuttin' t'say.
I t'ought t'meself
Screech is alright.
But a little too much

Vill muck up
er sight.
I'as me h'eyes came
ccustomed to
'wind h'an d'snow

s dis what 'tis like
When yer mind starts t'go?

I t'ought fer d'minit
Dat me noggin' come loose
But dere was a punt
Pulled by h'eight 'ardy moose.

An' a fat little skipper
Wit a h'oar in 'ee's 'and

'Ee was scullin' d'punt
From d' h'ice to d'land

Now Brian I won't cod ya
You 'ave a long 'aul,
But Romkey will 'elp ya
Hit over dis squal.
An' Cretchin is wit us
An' 'elp ya' 'ee will
So keep pullin' dis punt
To d'top of d'ill.

Depend on our Chuck, 'ee's fass an' 'ee's loose,
An' our Decker fears, neider man nor d' moose.

To d'top of d'shed
An' den h'onto d'roofs
You could tell dey was h'up dere
By d'sound of d'oofs.

Den h'over d'loft
Dere rose such a clatter
An' I t'ought what
might happen h'if
Dem moose was much
fatter!

I was feared fer a second
D'shingles might peel
From d'scrapin' an'
scratchin' of d'big punt's keel.

Den down tru d'chimney
D' h'ole skipper 'ee came ...

An' of course
It was Santa —
To use 'ee's right name.

Den h'out in
D'front room
A black cloud arose
D'soot looked like spume
From a whale
When she blows.

’Ee stood fer a minit
To Size h’up d’place

Wit black soot an’ h’ashes
All h’over ’ee’s face.

I t'ought to meself
H'as I gawked at d'man
What fine sealskin mittens
'Ee 'ad on ee's 'ands.

An' glossy new gumboots
To cover 'ee's feet
I couldn't imagine
'Ow 'ee kept 'em so neat.

E 'AD A SOU'WESTER WHO'S COLOR WAS RED
N' DIS 'EE 'AD PERCHED ON D'BACK OF 'EE'S 'EAD
IT' DEM FINE RED H'OIL SKINS LIKE I NEVER SAW AFORE
AT FITTED TOO TIGHT AN' REACHED DOWN TO D'FLOOR.

'Ee's face it was worn
An' weathered an' wrinkled
But 'ee's sparklin' blue h'eyes'
Still 'eld to der twinkle.

An' now when I looked
I saw naught but 'ee's back

H'as 'ee wrestled and juggled
D'gifts in 'ee's sack.

Den to d'mantle h'as 'ee lifted d'sox
H'apples an' h'ranges an' small toys in a box.

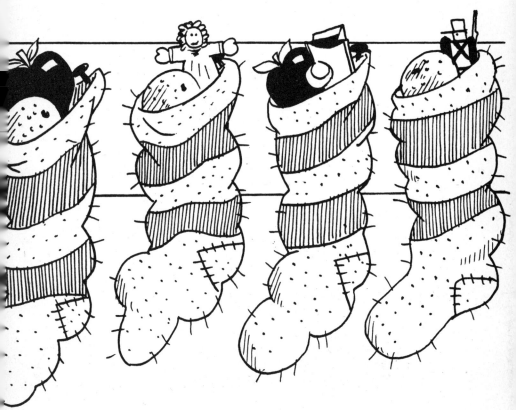

'Ee topped h'off each one
Fer d'garls h'an' d'b'ys

Wit' a small bag of bulls eyes
an' small wooden toys.

'Ee looked so 'appy an' jolly an' fine
H'as 'ee took a great gulp of dogberry wine.

'Ee tasted d'fruit cake and den figgy duff
Den 'ee spoke to 'eeself'
"Dis sure is fine stuff!"

'Ee tied h'up d'sack
Wit' a big granny knot
Den rested 'ee's 'ands
On d'top of 'ee's pot.

Now to d'chimney
Ee went wit a dash,
H'as ee's h'eyes crossed d'room
Wit' a flicker an' flash,
Now sure I must say
Dat 'ee cut a fine figger.

H'as 'ee slipped h'up d'chimeny
Like a bright squid jigger

'Ee walked cross d'roof
Back to d'front
An' I feared 'ee might slip
H'as 'ee got in d'punt.

Den down tru d'garden
An' h'onto d'bay
Midst d'clammer of 'oofs
I 'eard 'im say:

'Tis another year gone
God Bless you an' yours
May "ee grant you ...
FAIR WINDS
As you bend at d'oars.

A MERRY

A VERY MERRY

CHRISTMAS TO ALL YOUSE